the MONITOR meets the MERRIMACK

by Raymond P. Hill

Orlando   Austin   Chicago   New York   Toronto   London   San Diego

Visit *The Learning Site!*
www.harcourtschool.com

The date was Saturday, March 8, 1862. It was like an early spring day in Virginia. The sailors on the Union warships anchored in Hampton Roads were enjoying the afternoon sun. Some performed their duties. Others washed their uniforms, napped, or wrote letters. Everything was peaceful that afternoon. It didn't stay that way for long.

The Civil War had been underway for 11 months. The Southern states had broken away from the United States of America and formed their own country, the Confederate States of America. The Northern states, known as the Union, were trying to crush the Confederacy. Virginia was a Confederate state. In fact, Richmond, Virginia, was the capital of the Confederacy.

Union forces had controlled part of eastern Virginia since the spring of 1861. That part included a section of Hampton Roads, a bay leading directly to the Atlantic Ocean. In 1862 Confederate forces had control of the southern edge of Hampton Roads. The Elizabeth River and the city of Norfolk were in Confederate hands. The Union forces held the northern edge of the bay and, with it, the mouth of the James River. The Union warships were anchored close to the northern shore. There, they were protected by artillery in the hills above them. The ships also were out of range of the Confederate army guns sitting above the Elizabeth River.

The Union ships formed a naval blockade. They blocked Confederate ships in Virginia from reaching the Atlantic Ocean. The blockade prevented goods made by Virginians from being sold overseas. It also prevented Confederate and foreign vessels from taking food and weapons into Virginia.

This map of Virginia shows the Hampton Roads area.

The USS *Unadilla* was one of the Union ships that blockaded the ports of the Confederacy. Sailors on wooden ships like this one would soon face ships with sides made of metal.

Iron Against Wood

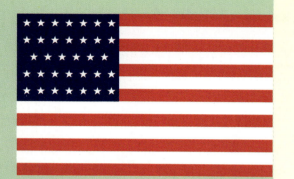

In 1862, the stars on the United States flag (above) represented all 34 states. The stars on the Confederate flag (below) represented the original seven Confederate states.

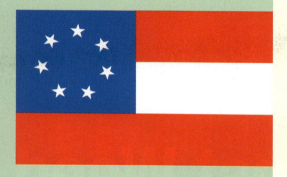

The Confederacy was desperate to end the blockade, but the Union fleet included five large, heavily armed warships. The Rebels (a Northern term for Confederates) had no warships powerful enough to defeat them. That was about to change.

On that lazy Saturday morning, the Union sailors became alert when they heard the shouts of lookouts. The lookouts pointed south, in the direction of the Elizabeth River. They saw something very strange. It looked like a long, black barn floating out of the mouth of the river and into the bay. This "barn" had a big smokestack belching smoke. Behind the smokestack was a tall flagpole, and waving from it was a red, white, and blue Confederate flag. The strange object was the Rebel ironclad *Merrimack*.

A wooden ship called the *Merrimack* was covered with iron and renamed the *Virginia*. However, most people today still call the *Virginia* by its original name—the *Merrimack*.

The *Merrimack* had a very unusual history. The vessel had once been a Union warship. In April 1861 the Union army had deliberately burned and sunk the wooden *Merrimack* to prevent the Confederates from capturing the vessel. Later, the Confederates raised the *Merrimack* and changed it into an ironclad. The *Merrimack* was still made of wood below the waterline. Above the waterline, every inch of the ship was covered with black iron plates four inches (10 cm) thick.

Until that day, hardly any ironclad ships had been used in America. Even the most powerful steam-powered warships had wooden hulls. The Union sailors had never seen anything like this unusual vessel.

In April 1861, retreating Union soldiers in Portsmouth, Virginia, set fire to the Gosport Navy Yard and 11 warships, including the *Merrimack*. This was to keep the ships out of the hands of the Confederates.

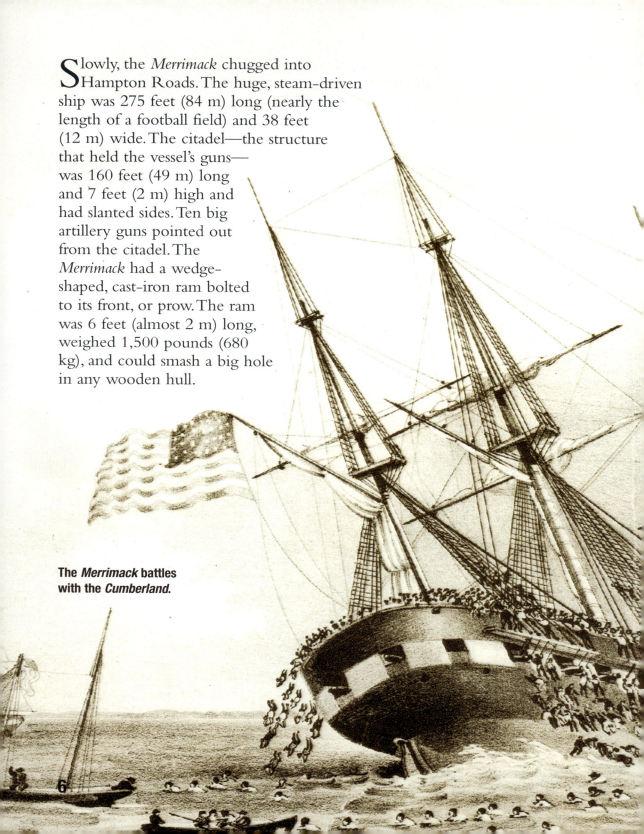

Slowly, the *Merrimack* chugged into Hampton Roads. The huge, steam-driven ship was 275 feet (84 m) long (nearly the length of a football field) and 38 feet (12 m) wide. The citadel—the structure that held the vessel's guns—was 160 feet (49 m) long and 7 feet (2 m) high and had slanted sides. Ten big artillery guns pointed out from the citadel. The *Merrimack* had a wedge-shaped, cast-iron ram bolted to its front, or prow. The ram was 6 feet (almost 2 m) long, weighed 1,500 pounds (680 kg), and could smash a big hole in any wooden hull.

The *Merrimack* battles with the *Cumberland*.

The Confederate ironclad slowly moved toward two Union ships anchored at the mouth of the James River. It took a while to reach them. With a weight of 3,200 tons, the ironclad could barely make a speed of less than ten knots. Four strong sailors were needed to turn the ship's steering wheel to change course.

Inside the ironclad, it was hot and noisy for the crew of 320 men, but the Confederates were eager to fight. One crewman wrote about what happened when the Yankees (a Southern term for Northerners) first saw the ironclad. "As we rounded into view, the white-winged sailing craft . . . scurried to the far shore like chickens on the approach of a hovering hawk."

The *Merrimack* closed in on a Union warship, the USS *Congress*, which opened fire. One officer on the Union ship said that the shells bounced off the *Merrimack*'s armor like "water from a duck's back." Then the *Merrimack*'s guns roared back, and her shells tore big holes in the wooden vessel.

Meanwhile, Union guns along the banks of the bay fired at the *Merrimack*, but the cannonballs bounced off the ship. Other Union ships tried to get into the fight, but many of them, including the USS *Minnesota*, became stuck on sandbars in shallow water.

The *Merrimack* went after a Union warship several hundred yards away. As it came close to the USS *Cumberland*, the *Merrimack* was hit by the *Cumberland*'s shells. One shell cut the *Merrimack*'s anchor chain. The giant chain whipped around inside the ship, killing two crewmen and injuring several others.

The *Merrimack* caused the Union to suffer almost 400 casualties (killed, wounded, and missing sailors).

The *Merrimack* rammed the front of the *Cumberland* below the waterline. It made a hole in the hull, said one witness, "big enough to drive a horse and buggy through." The *Cumberland* quickly started to sink, taking the *Merrimack* with it. The ironclad's ram was stuck in the hull!

The *Merrimack*'s commander, Franklin Buchanan, reversed the engines so the ship could back out of the hole. The *Cumberland* kept firing at the *Merrimack*, causing a leak in the ironclad. The firing stopped as the *Cumberland* sank in 54 feet (16 m) of water.

Now the *Congress* moved into shallower waters to escape the *Merrimack*. The *Congress* became stuck on a sandbar. The *Merrimack* blasted the trapped Union vessel, setting it on fire. Finally, the *Congress* raised a white flag of surrender. After the crew left the ship, the fire set off gunpowder on the *Congress*, and the ship exploded.

Buchanan, the captain of the *Merrimack*, had been hit by a bullet while walking on deck. Lieutenant Catesby R. Jones took over command of the ship. With the ship leaking, Jones decided to take the *Merrimack* back to Norfolk.

It was obvious that the Union's wooden warships were no match for the *Merrimack*. Could the Rebel ironclad do as well in a fight with a Yankee ironclad? The world was about to find out.

Franklin Buchanan

The Union had an ironclad called the *Monitor*, and it was under the command of Lieutenant John L. Worden. The vessel steamed into Hampton Roads after sundown on March 8, 1862, but it arrived too late to fight the *Merrimack*.

Except for their black armor, the *Monitor* and the *Merrimack* were very different. The deck of the *Monitor* was only 13 inches (33 cm) above the waterline. Most of the ship and nearly all of its crew of 58 were below the waterline.

The *Monitor* was much smaller than the *Merrimack*. The Yankee ironclad was 172 feet (52 m) long and 41 feet (12 m) wide and weighed 776 tons. It carried only two guns, both in a round, revolving turret that was 9 feet (3 m) high and 20 feet (6 m) across. In front of the turret was a 3-foot-high (1-m-high) iron box. From inside the vessel, the captain could view a battle through a slit in the box. Also on the *Monitor*'s deck was a smokestack that could be lowered during combat.

The *Monitor* had been designed by John Ericsson, a brilliant Swedish inventor. It was built at the Brooklyn, New York, naval yard and rushed to Hampton Roads to face the *Merrimack*. Five days after it sailed from Brooklyn, the *Monitor* arrived in Virginia.

On Sunday morning, March 9, 1862, Northern and Southern soldiers on both sides of the bay watched the *Merrimack* arrive. Confederate workers had stayed up all night repairing the *Merrimack*. On the Union side, tugboats had spent the night trying to tow the USS *Minnesota* off a sandbar. With 44 guns, it was one of the most powerful vessels in the Union navy. Now it was a sitting target.

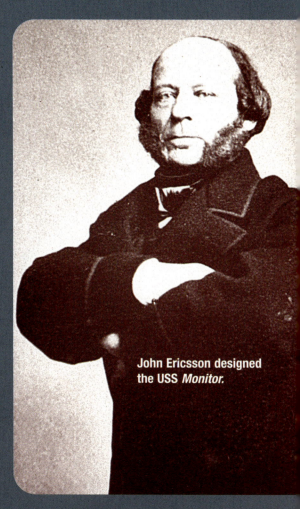

John Ericsson designed the USS *Monitor*.

TFK IRONCLAD FACTS

- It took the Confederacy nine months and $110,000 to raise the wooden *Merrimack* and make it into an ironclad. The *Monitor* was built from scratch in four months for $195,000 in private funds.

- The United States navy had condemned the engines of the wooden *Merrimack* as unfit for service. The Confederacy had no choice but to use those same engines in the much-heavier ironclad *Merrimack*.

- The *Monitor* was rushed into service before it could be commissioned as a United States warship. Three civilians had paid for and owned the *Monitor* at the time of its fight with the *Merrimack*.

- The South did not have experienced sailors. Most of the 320 men on the ironclad *Merrimack* were volunteers from the Confederate army.

- The *Minnesota*, one of the vessels attacked by the ironclad *Merrimack*, was a sister ship of the wooden *Merrimack*.

Ericsson named his vessel the *Monitor* because he believed it would make the nation's enemies behave themselves.

Iron Against Iron

When the *Merrimack* closed in on the *Minnesota,* the *Monitor* came to its rescue. One officer on the *Minnesota* described the start of the battle. He said, "Gun after gun was fired by the *Monitor,* which was returned with whole broadsides by the rebel with no more effect, apparently, than so many pebble-stones thrown by a child."

The *Monitor* was faster and easier to steer and turn than the *Merrimack,* and its armor was twice as thick as the *Merrimack*'s. At one point, the two ships were only a few yards apart as they fired nonstop at each other. The most they did was dent each other's iron surfaces.

"The *Merrimack* couldn't sink us if we let her pound us for a month!" Worden shouted to his crew. Of course, the *Monitor* couldn't do much damage to the *Merrimack,* either.

During the battle, the *Merrimack* began to fire shells at the *Minnesota*. The Confederate ship damaged the *Minnesota* and sank a Union tugboat. Fighting back, the *Minnesota* blasted the *Merrimack*. This rocked the Southern ironclad but didn't harm it.

Turning away from the *Minnesota,* the *Merrimack* tried to ram the *Monitor*. The Northern ironclad dodged it, receiving a glancing blow. As it tried to hit the *Monitor* again, the *Merrimack* became stuck in shallow water. The ship could not move!

The *Monitor* had no problems in shallow water. The draft, or part of the ship below the waterline, was only 10 feet (3 m). The *Merrimack*'s draft was 22 feet (7 m). The *Monitor* tried to ram and cripple the *Merrimack*'s propeller. The blow missed the propeller.

The *Merrimack* fired at the *Monitor* as the Union ship steamed by. One shell hit the *Monitor*'s protected pilothouse. Gunpowder and tiny bits of iron hit Worden's face, hurting the captain's eyes. Lieutenant Samuel Dana Greene took command of the *Monitor*. In the confusion, the ship began to move away from the *Merrimack*.

Meanwhile, the *Merrimack* tried to pull itself off the sandbar. H. Ashton Ramsay, the ship's chief engineer, ordered the crew to throw oil-soaked rags into the furnaces to increase the heat and produce more steam. "We lashed down the safety valves . . . and brought the boilers to a pressure that would have been unsafe under ordinary circumstances," Ramsey recalled. Slowly, inch by inch, the Confederate vessel pulled itself out of the mud.

Now the two ironclads were far apart. The *Merrimack*'s acting captain, Catesby Jones, worried about the shallow waters around the *Minnesota*. He called off the fight. As the *Merrimack* headed for Norfolk, Lieutenant Greene guided the *Monitor* back to protect the *Minnesota*. The first battle of ironclad ships in history was over.

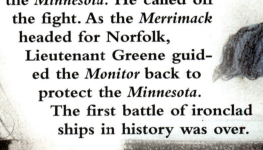

Most of the shells fired by the *Merrimack* passed harmlessly over the flat deck of the *Monitor*.

The two vessels had dueled for four and a half hours with no real winner. Neither ship was sunk, but some historians give the edge to the *Monitor*. After all, the *Merrimack* had failed to break the blockade at Hampton Roads.

The *Merrimack* fought no more battles. Two months later, Union forces were about to capture eastern Virginia. The Confederates blew up the *Merrimack* on May 11, 1862, to prevent the ship from falling into enemy hands.

The *Monitor* sank in a storm off Cape Hatteras, North Carolina, on December 31, 1862.

The Confederacy built at least 40 more ironclads during the Civil War. The Union built 60 more of them. After the war, the United States stopped building wooden warships. The age of the iron warship had begun.

In 1862 the Union used the *Carondelet*, the *Pittsburgh*, and other ironclads to attack a Confederate fort on the Mississippi River.

In 1991, the USS *Missouri* launched missiles against Iraq in the Persian Gulf War.

TFK FAST FACTS

Famous Warships of the United States

BONHOMME RICHARD—In 1779 the *Bonhomme Richard* was rebuilt from a French ship for John Paul Jones, a great American naval captain of the Revolutionary War. With Jones in command, the *Bonhomme Richard* fought and defeated a British warship named the *Serapis*. During the fight, the captain of the *Serapis* asked Jones to surrender. Jones answered, "I have not yet begun to fight."

USS CONSTELLATION—This was the first ship commissioned, or ordered to be built, by the United States Navy. It was also the first warship built in the United States to fight, defeat, and capture an enemy. Launched in 1797, it won several sea battles in a short war against France. The *Constellation* also fought in the War of 1812.

USS CONSTITUTION—In the War of 1812, the *Constitution* fought a sea battle against a British ship. When the British shells bounced off the wooden hull of the *Constitution,* it became known as Old Ironsides. The *Constitution* never lost a battle at sea.

USS MISSOURI—Launched in 1944, this was the last battleship built by the United States Navy. In World War II, the *Missouri* fought in the Pacific Ocean, supporting troops in the invasions of Iwo Jima and Okinawa. The ship also bombarded targets on the Japanese mainland. Japan and the United States signed the surrender treaty on the deck of the *Missouri* in 1945.

Scientists and navy divers bring up the steam engine of the *Monitor*. The engine is now on display at The Mariners' Museum in Newport News, Virginia.

TFK FAST FACTS

Monitor National Marine Sanctuary

- In 1973 the wreck of the *Monitor* was found 16 miles (26 km) from the lighthouse at Cape Hatteras, North Carolina. The ship was resting on the bottom of the sea, 235 feet (72 m) below the surface.
- In 1975 the United States declared the resting place of the *Monitor* a marine sanctuary. No one is allowed within a mile (about 1.5 km) of the ship without permission.
- The *Monitor* is in such bad shape that it cannot be raised to the surface in one piece. Instead, divers are bringing up pieces of the ship, such as its engine and propellers.